Mary Magdalene and the Gardener
Women Leaders in the Church

Brian Lennon SJ

With a Foreword by Ruth Patterson

Published by Messenger Publications, 2021

ISBN 978 1 78812 314 3

Designed by Messenger Publications Design Department
Typeset in Adobe Caslon Pro & Calluna
Printed by Baird W & G Ltd

Messenger Publications,
37 Leeson Place, Dublin D02 E5V0
www.messenger.ie

CONTENTS

FOREWORD

Mary Magdalene fascinates me. Whenever you do a brief reconnoitre of the gospels it's astonishing how often her name crops up. Yet, it has taken many centuries for us to move beyond a two-dimensional image and, with dawning awareness, recognise that here indeed is the apostle to the apostles. The implications of such awareness have, by and large, yet to be acknowledged. This encounter with the Gardener on Easter morning is the culmination of a journey of loving companionship, one that encouraged Mary to emerge out of the cocoon of a particular way of thinking and being that had been the totality of her faith experience (both scriptural and traditional) and soar into a new world of awareness. All this Brian Lennon unfolds for us in this challenging and hope-filled meditation.

At the close Brian writes, 'One word had transformed the world, "Mary"'. A few years ago at a conference I heard someone say, 'Nothing less than Infinite Love has the power to name who you are'. In that garden it was Infinite Love that cleared Mary's vision and led to recognition. It was Infinite

Love that had drawn her in the first place, that had encouraged her into an ever-deepening communion, that shaped and formed her spirituality, that enabled her to remain steadfast and that empowered her to respond to the commission to go and tell the Good News that 'Christ has died; Christ has risen; Christ will come again'.

It is the 'overwhelming love revealed in the voice of the Gardener' that restores hope, makes all things new and everything possible. Brian presents us with this challenge when he writes, 'In the end the Voice confronts us with a choice: to listen to the whisper or to stay within the limits of our sight'. It is not too much to say that upon our choice rests the future of this planet, and indeed the future of our Church with particular reference to the place of women, which Mary Magdalene exemplifies.

To move beyond the limits of our sight, of how things have always been perceived, to listen and respond to the whisper, to be part of a world where margins become centres and where everything belongs is to be open to Infinite Love.

Ruth Patterson

Ruth Patterson was the first woman to be ordained to the ministry of the Presbyterian Church in Ireland and is the director of Restoration Ministries

PART 1

MARY'S STORY

On the surface the encounter of Mary with the Gardener seems to be a simple resurrection story, but of course that is a contradiction. There are no simple resurrection stories, since resurrections do not happen.

That at least is the way it appears to millions, and that certainly is the way it appeared to Mary early that morning when she went to the place where they had buried her murdered rabbi. She saw that the stone in front of the grave had been moved.

She knew immediately what this meant: the grave had been robbed.

As a Jew she knew that resurrections do not happen. She probably believed that there would be a resurrection from the dead for those faithful to God's law. But this would only take place at the end of the world, whenever that would be. She knew what they had done to her rabbi. She had seen it, from afar.

The Crucifixion and the Empty Tomb

She had seen plenty of other crucifixions. They were one of the means used by the Roman occupiers of Palestine to keep order. Normally it involved scourging, probably administered by two soldiers with a whip with fairly short cords on it. Sharp pieces of bone were tied to the end of each cord, and these flayed the back of the prisoner, often until the bones of the spine were showing. The soldiers had to be careful not to overdo it: they did not want the prisoner to become unconscious, or to die. They had more in store for him.

They then pulled the prisoner out of the barracks and made him carry one large piece of wood on his back. If he didn't, he got kicked, and was whipped again. Usually there was no trouble with onlookers: in the case of the rabbi most were too busy preparing for the Sabbath, which was a special one. For the onlookers, there was nothing remarkable about yet one more crucifixion. After all, this rabbi was a troublemaker: he must have known what he was bringing on himself.

When they got to Golgotha – part of a rubbish dump just outside the walls of the city – they stripped him naked, nailed his wrists to the plank he had carried, hauled it onto an upright plank left standing from the last victim, and then nailed his feet to the upright.

Pilate, the Roman governor, had told them to nail a notice to the top of the cross: 'Jesus of Nazareth, King of the Jews', and this they did. Crucifixions were done to teach people: this is what will happen to you if you get ideas above your station.

Often people took a while to die: sometimes even a few days. But the rabbi died comparatively quickly. The victim could hold himself up by his nailed feet for only so long. As he grew weaker his body began to slump. He could no longer lift his head to breathe, so he began to choke. After a few moments he would make another effort and lift his head again to breathe. But the longer this went on the more difficult it became. In the end he choked slowly to death.

All this Mary had observed from afar. When she saw the rabbi butchered, despite the agony that this caused her, she did not turn away. Instead, after they had taken the body down from the cross, she watched as they put it in an empty tomb and rolled a great big stone across the entrance.

Early on the morning following the Sabbath, when Jewish law required her to stay at home, she came with spices to anoint the body.

Some Gospel accounts suggest that she was with some other women, some that she was on her own. At no point do the women seem to have asked how they would roll back the heavy stone in front of the grave: they certainly could not have done this on their own. As it happened, when Mary got to the grave it was already open.

As we have seen, her immediate reaction was that the grave had been robbed. Indeed, the rabbi, while alive, had said some strange things about rising from the dead. He had said a lot of strange things. It was not surprising that some of those who had wanted to kill him had robbed the body.

She ran back to the other disciples. They were locked in a house because they were afraid for their lives. She told them what had happened. Peter and the 'beloved disciple' ran back to the tomb with her, saw that she had been telling the truth, and then went back to their safe house.

While standing at the tomb, weeping, Mary saw two angels. She knew the stories of angels in her Jewish Scriptures. She was deeply upset, so seeing visions of angels might not be unexpected.

They asked her, 'Why are you crying?' The answer seems obvious. Why would anyone be crying outside a grave? – because he or she has lost someone. Nonetheless, she answered them, 'They have taken my Lord away, and I don't know where they have put him'.

Meeting the Gardener

At that point she turned around and saw the Gardener standing behind her. He asked the same question: 'Why are you crying?' Since no one else was around Mary came to the obvious conclusion that it was he who had robbed the body. She said, 'If you took him away, sir, tell me where you have put him, and I will go and get him'. Then she turned back to look into the empty grave.

Mary's response was coloured by her grief: if the Gardener had taken the body he was not likely to tell her where he had put it. Even if he did tell her, how could she carry the dead weight of a thirty-year-old man?

At that point a single word was spoken. It was spoken by the Gardener, and was addressed to Mary's back.

It was a single word that has exploded into the world like a nuclear bomb, because if this story is true then the speaking of that word has changed everything.

It changed Mary's own life totally. It changed

the lives of his followers, but it also changed the lives of those who killed him, and the lives of you and of me.

The one word spoken was her name.

There was only one person in the world who could speak Mary's name in the way the Gardener did, but he was dead. Yet he had spoken her name.

This is where letters on a page cannot help us: we have to hear the word spoken. Perhaps the best analogy is from a phone call: 'Hello, it's me'. There are a lot of people answering to 'me' in the world. Indeed, as a write, I am just off the phone from my one-and-a-half-year-old grand-nephew who tells me he's 'me'. We never ask them who they are. We know who they are as soon as we hear their voice.

The word was spoken. She knew him then. Four words, but, short as they are, they point to the change that went on within Mary. However many words we use ourselves we can only point to intimations of what happened inside Mary. Her rabbi had been butchered. He had been ripped away from her. All his talk – dream talk – about making a new world, about forgiving and understanding, respect and freedom, and all the rest of that stuff was gone. The dream was over. His presence had been replaced with emptiness and pain. The light had gone out.

Yet the word had been spoken, the word that shattered every obvious reality. It meant that the Gardener was alive, that he had overcome death. The butchery had not been the end of the story. Of course, all this was impossible, because the resurrection of a man before the last day was impossible. Clearly the Gardener was a ghost, except that he did not look like a ghost. When Mary flung herself at his feet, they seemed real, when she looked he was there, and she had heard her name spoken in the way only one person in the world could speak it.

The word spoken was her name. For Jews, one's name is a symbol, a pointer to the person's full reality. In speaking it, the Gardener was entering into her history, her pain, her vulnerability, her hopes and fears, her dreams, her joys: all the utterly complex reality that is a human person; all summed up in that one word.

We don't know when Mary had first come across the Gardener. The gospels tell us that he had cast out seven demons from her. The Gardener, while he was alive, had a reputation for healing, but we are not told what her illness was. The gospels make clear that, while physical healing mattered to him, what followed was even more important. In Mary's case what followed changed her life.

She had loved the rabbi so much that she became his disciple, along with other women, and some men. Becoming his disciple meant that she left her home and followed him. This would not have been her family's plan for her. Women were worth money: when they married, the groom's family paid a dowry. That mattered in a society where money was tight. Following the rabbi meant there was no dowry. Leaving home to become his disciple meant, if not breaking with her family, at least a major row, but she never showed any sign of regretting her decision.

The story mentions that Mary turned around twice: first when she faced into the tomb, and the Gardener, standing behind her, asked why she was weeping. She turned to ask him her own question about where he had put the body. Then she must have turned back towards the tomb again, because we are told that when he spoke her name she turned back to him a second time and embraced his feet. The image may be stressing that Mary turned away from the grave, from death, towards life: incredible new life. In part this is about one man being alive instead of dead, but it is also about much more than that.

After having spoken her name, the Gardener said something more. Something that seems even more out of place than his question to Mary at the grave, 'Why are you crying?'. He said, 'Do not cling to me'. What did he expect her to do? He knew how much she loved him. He knew that she had suffered brutally watching his suffering and death. Now that he had spoken her name, thereby transforming darkness and despair into incredible hope, what did he expect her to do? Yet he said, 'Do not cling to me'.

The reason that the Gardener told her not to cling to him was that he had not yet gone back to his Father. Speaking her name meant that he had overcome death, that he was alive. But this did not mean that everything would go back to what it had been before his death. This pointed to a reality that was difficult: his death had changed their relationship. But it pointed to something else that was even more important: his death had not ended their relationship. In fact, by the power of his Spirit, his death was going to deepen their relationship in ways that she could not imagine.

By grasping his feet Mary was holding on to the rabbi she had loved, lost and found again. While he was the same rabbi, he was also different. The

Gardener was not like Lazarus, whom he had raised from the dead, and who in due course would die again. The Gardener would never die again. He was now glorified. In that glory he was being reunited with his Father, his 'Abba'. Mary now had to learn how to relate to him in a new way.

The Gardener and His Abba

Going to the Father was a pointer to something. All through his life one of the two passions of the Gardener was his love for his God whom he called 'Abba' – a modern translation might be 'Daddy'. So, when the Gardener talked of 'going back to the Father' he was pointing back to a central passion of his life, but he was also pointing forward to something.

It would take many centuries before his followers found words for what he was talking about. Inevitably these were poor words: the union of the Father, Son and Holy Spirit, Three Persons in One God, utterly in love with each other and with every person in the world.

Mary's clinging to the Gardener's feet was not only an expression of the overwhelming love she felt for him, it was doing something else: she was worshipping him. That might not have been in her mind at the time of the original event, but it was certainly in the gospel author's mind when he wrote this story sixty years after the event. That is why he has Mary say 'They have taken my Lord' (John 20:13).

Worship is due only to God, not to anyone else. Worship is about bowing down in awe before someone who is beyond us; someone whom we do not understand; who is completely transcendent; who is mystery. More: one who is mystery, not in the sense of something to be puzzled out, but rather as someone so deep that we can never plumb his or her depths.

Later, when the other disciples went through the same experience as Mary, and moved from despair and absolute disbelief to an overwhelming hope, they noticed one pattern in all their stories: the Gardener always took the initiative. It was always he who revealed himself. They could not arrange when he would make himself known. When he did, it always came as a surprise and filled them with awe and fear.

We are told several times – in this scene, in the Emmaus story (Luke 24) and in the story of the miracle of the fishes (John 21) – that they did not recognise him until he revealed himself. He had already spoken words to Mary, but she also did not recognise him. She only did so when he spoke her name.

There may be an echo in this of a much earlier story which all Jews knew well: the call of Moses. Yahweh calls Moses by name. Moses is in the desert, looking after his father-in-law's sheep when he hears the voice, but he does not know who is calling him. Yahweh has to tell him, 'I am the God of your father, the God of Abraham, the God of Isaac and the God of Jacob' (Exodus 3:6).

Moses, too, would become intimate with Yahweh. We are told that when he went to the tent of meeting he spoke to Yahweh 'as one speaks to a friend' (Exodus 33:11). Yet although Yahweh revealed himself as a pillar of cloud, or as thunder and lightning, or as a still, small voice (1 Kings 19:12), Yahweh did not show his face. God in Christ showed his face to Mary and she recognised him after he spoke her name.

A Friend, but Not Equal

Moses and Mary both saw themselves as friends of God. But that friendship was not one between equals. Both showed great intimacy: Moses arguing with Yahweh when Yahweh threatens to destroy the people, Mary being healed by the compassionate Gardener, looking desperately for his body, clinging to his feet in the garden. However, the relationships are not ordinary friendships.

In normal friendships we take on obligations: we care for each other, we are there when the other is in trouble, we reveal ourselves to the other, thereby making ourselves vulnerable, we laugh and do things together, we need each other.

All these were present in the friendship between Mary and her rabbi, but there was a difference: the Gardener was the same as other people, but he was also different: 'the Father and I are one' (John 10:30). The word spoken to Mary was spoken by her friend, but he is also her rabbi, her Messiah, and, more, he is the Son of the Father and is one with the Father and the Holy Spirit. The word was not only bringing her back into relationship with the Messiah, whom she had come to love, it was also drawing her into the depths of the love of the Father, the Son and the Holy Spirit. A love from which she, like all of us, had come, and to which she would return.

There is a further difference between Moses meeting Yahweh and Mary meeting the Gardener.

Moses stands between Yahweh and the people. He brought the message of Yahweh to the people. As we have mentioned, he argued with Yahweh in order to protect the people from Yahweh's anger. While Mary met the Gardener as directly as Moses met Yahweh, and while she also brought the Gardener's message to others, these others met the Gardener directly in due course. They did not have to go through Mary.

Covenant

As a Jew, Mary would almost certainly have known about God's Covenant: the agreement that God had made to be the God of the chosen people. For their part, the people were to keep God's law written in the Jewish Scriptures. However, time and again they shattered the Covenant as they turned away from the law: they went after idols, they mistreated the weak, widows and orphans, strangers and foreigners. God always threatened to destroy them, but always relented. Again and again God came back to the people with a new Covenant. Again and again they broke it and the cycle started over.

The word spoken by the Gardener broke this cycle. The Gardener, as a faithful Jew, one of God's chosen people, had been faithful to the Covenant. He had lived his life to the full. He had faced into the depths of defeat and darkness, torture and abandonment, and in response he had done two things. He had continued to speak the word of truth, and he had continued to trust in his 'Abba'. The cry of despair, 'My God, my God, why have you abandoned me?', had been followed by, 'Into thy hands I commend my spirit'. The Gardener had done what no other human had done: he had been faithful to the end, and he had trusted his God.

The rescue of the people from destroying themselves by idolatry and hatred had been completed, despite the long history of failure. Love had conquered fear, betrayal, bitterness and hopelessness.

Thus, in the Gardener, the Covenant had finally been fulfilled. The Gardener represented every person who had ever existed and he had been faithful to the last. The word that he spoke to Mary showed that he was alive, that God had affirmed him, that his life and suffering had not been in vain, that God had renewed the Covenant with God's people, but this time forever.

One word, 'Mary', shattered the power of evil and symbolised the victory of love.

The Mission

None of this was clear to Mary at the time. Instead she heard another word, and this word was a mission. The Gardener told her to go to his brothers and tell them that he was returning to his Father. He added something else, and this, together with the fact that he called them his 'brothers', was important. He said that he was returning to my Father *and to their Father*, to my God *and to their God*.

So, Mary's mission was twofold:

a. To tell them that he was alive, and
b. To tell them that they were restored to his friendship and were still sons of his Abba.

The meeting between Mary and the Gardener took place in the context of brokenness: the broken body on the cross and the broken relationships between the rabbi and his male disciples. They had all failed the test: when his hour came, when he was taken and crucified, they fled. One denied him explicitly. One betrayed him. Denial, treachery, disloyalty: these all break relationships. Yet the message Mary was told to bring to them was that despite all this they were still his 'brothers'. They were still sons of his Father. Despite all they had done, the relationships that had been shattered were now restored. The Gardener was telling Mary to tell his brothers about the depths of his Abba's forgiveness.

Mary would not have to protect the people from the anger of the Gardener, as Moses had done with Yahweh. The Gardener revealed what Yahweh is really like. The Gardener's response to the men's failure was not one of anger or vengeance. Instead he revealed himself to them, and treated them with loving compassion. He did not refer back to their total failure, except on one occasion: when the disciples met the stranger on the shore (John 21). Then the Gardener reminded Simon Peter of his denial, and did so three times. On each occasion he gave Simon a mission. The purpose of the dialogue is not to harangue Simon, but to show him that not only was he restored to friendship with the Gardener, he was also given increased responsibility to spread the good news that God is a loving God, full of tenderness and compassion: 'As a mother comforts her child, so I will comfort you' (Isaiah 66:13).

It speaks volumes for Mary first that she was given this mission, and secondly that she tore herself away from her rabbi and carried it out. She went to the disciples, told them that she had seen the Lord, and that he had said these things to her.

In Luke's version of the story the disciples did not believe her. They knew that she was talking nonsense, because men do not rise from the dead and because in the culture of the time women were considered emotional. Mary was seeing ghosts and talking the sort of nonsense that one might expect from a woman. John tells us that the beloved disciple, who followed Mary back to the tomb with Peter, 'saw and believed'. He tells us nothing about the response of the others. Given this it seems unlikely that they reacted any differently from Thomas, who rejected the story when the other men told him. It seems likely that Mary failed in her mission: most of the men did not believe her.

PART 2

UNDERSTANDING MARY'S STORY

The story is a wonderful one. But is it true? It was written around AD 90, about sixty years after the death of the Gardener. Mary, assuming she was at least twenty at the time of his death, was surely well dead by this time: average life expectancy was around thirty. The story is not history as we understand it. Like all the gospel stories it is trying to tell us something about how God was revealed in the Gardener.

Did It Happen?

One of the criteria used by scholars to judge the likelihood of a gospel story having actually taken place is to see how many gospels include some version of it: if it occurs in several gospels, and they are also able to show that it came from different traditions, then they think it more likely that something like the events described really took place.

In this case a version of the story appears in Mark (chapter 16) and Matthew (chapter 28), as well as in John's Gospel. Mark and Matthew's stories may have come from a tradition different from that used by John. John also changes many of the details: only he refers to the Gardener greeting Mary by name and her clinging to him. Despite these differences in details, the story passes the test of coming from multiple sources, and of appearing in several gospels.

It is also striking that this first appearance of the Gardener is to a woman. Women were not seen as equal to men. If, therefore, you were a gospel writer and wanted to convince people of the resurrection, the more obvious strategy would be to pick a man as your chief witness, but this is not what they did. They chose a woman.

All this suggests that something like these events actually happened.

We know nothing about Mary's life after her mission to the men. However, the fact that in almost all the New Testament stories she is listed as the first person to whom the Gardener appeared suggests that she remained very prominent in the community after the death of her rabbi.

We have mentioned the disbelief of the male

disciples in Luke's version when they were told about the resurrection. Apart from their view of women as prone to hysteria, they probably also assumed that Mary had seen a ghost. The possibility of seeing ghosts was part of the mental life of pre-modern people. The problem with this ghost was that he had spoken, that he had feet, that he ate and drank with them. Ghosts do not have feet. That is why, when the gospel writers came to write their stories they used the Greek word *anastasis* to describe the resurrection of the Gardener. This was not a word they used about ghosts: rather it was the one they used about the resurrection at the end of time when God's chosen would rise from the dead, body and soul.[1] Those Jews who believed in a resurrection from the dead believed that it could only happen at the end of time, not now. All those early disciples who accepted the resurrection went through a similar process of moving from absolute disbelief to belief.

The fact that the gospels tell us about the disbelief of the men, and in particular of the male leaders, reinforces the argument that something remarkable had happened. If you are writing a story to show how marvellous the rabbi is, and also how

1 Tom Wright, *Surprised by Hope*, London: SPCK, 2007, p.61.

reliable his followers are, you do not include stories that show these leaders in a bad light. Including Mary's story in their accounts suggests that the story was so widespread that the gospel writers could not avoid including it, and that it fitted in with their own experiences.

There is an argument against the reliability of the story: As we have seen, the gospel writers were not writing history in the modern sense. In the case of John his purpose was 'that you may come to believe that Jesus is the Messiah, the Son of God, and that through believing you may have life in his name' (John 20:31).

So perhaps the story is not literally true. When people hear this they often feel disappointed. More, they feel that their faith has been undermined: if they cannot believe that the gospel stories happened as described, how can they believe anything about their faith?

This question misses a really important point. No story can tell us what really happened.

Try telling someone else about your closest relationship; or try describing a person to whom you are really close to someone else. You can't do it. That is why we can find people talking about their spouses or children so boring: we cannot experience what they are talking about. However, stories can give us glimmers. We use these glimmers to connect with our own experiences, and that gives us some idea about what people are saying – but only some idea.

All the gospel stories tell us of the fear of the disciples when the rabbi is arrested. John tells us they were gathered in the upper room with the doors locked for fear of the Jewish leaders (John 20:19). Yet, some time after the death of the Gardener they were transformed from people cowering with fear to people going out into the public world, proclaiming that the rabbi had overcome death, and that everyone should follow him.

Given the danger that they were in from their own religious leaders and the Romans who had just crucified the rabbi because they saw him as a dangerous disturber of the peace, this was an incredibly brave act. It was also a remarkable transformation.

The early accounts all show the disciples pointing back to an experience they had had. Through this experience they became convinced that the rabbi was alive. The stories they told may not have happened in exactly the way that they told them, but *something* happened that transformed them, and they told these stories to give us some clues about what they went through.

The problem for the gospel writers was that the followers of the Gardener had gone through something literally unbelievable. They themselves – all of them – had not believed Mary's story. So, when they did go through the experience themselves how were they ever going to tell other people about it, since they in turn would disbelieve the story? In any case, no story could communicate what they had gone through.

The story of Mary and the Gardener may or may not be literally true – we actually have no way of knowing. What the story – and it is a wonderful story – does is to point our hearts beyond the story, to our own experience.

The Gardener reveals himself to Mary. She does not know him until this happens. That is always the case: all those who followed after Mary could only relate to the story, could only glimpse some of what it pointed towards, after the Gardener had revealed himself to them.

Why the Gardener reveals himself to some and not to others will always be a mystery. So also will be the timing. The Gardener had been drawing Mary to himself long before the meeting at the tomb. That is why Mary was up early in the morning looking for him so that she could anoint his body.

Dead Men Don't Talk

There is a further obvious problem with the story: dead men don't talk. The story can only make sense to those who are open to the idea of life after death. Secularists are clear: the body disintegrates after death. The brain disappears. Therefore, so also does the person.

There are some points that are worth considering in response. They are not counter-arguments that prove an afterlife, but rather pointers to something else.

Biologically, a peculiar thing about the human body is that most of its cells change completely about every seven to ten years. So, the old philosophical conundrum about the chair – if you change the feet, and the seat, and the back, do you have the same chair? – can be asked of humans. If you look at a photo of a baby, few outside her family will recognise the same person sixty years later. Yet, despite the physical changes, the ageing and the different cells, it is still the same person. Even if the brain declines with Alzheimer's, she is still the same person, although sadly diminished. Does this point to an afterlife? No, but it points to one central reality: our human reality is not encountered only in our bodies. The essence of our being is not visible to our eyes. Our bodies change, but we still remain the same person.

When she met the Gardener Mary knew that he was different. She also knew that he was the same person. Despite believing that no one could rise before the last day, she believed that he was alive. The disciples, equally certain in their disbelief, came to the same conclusion. So they were not talking about a corpse coming to life – none of the gospels mention anything like this. Instead they were saying that they had experienced their crucified Lord as being alive, still with the marks of crucifixion, clearly the same person that they had known, but equally clearly changed in ways that they could not easily describe.

Beauty, injustice and sacrifice all raise problems with the idea that everything ends with death.

Consider the beauty of a Beethoven piano sonata, the marvels of art, the efforts scientists make to overcome disease; or the marvels of relationships, love grown over years in good times and bad, leading to deep connections between people: is all this for nothing? Are photos, memories and genes all that we are left with?

Or consider the terrible injustices in the world: the Holocaust in which millions of Jews and Travellers, gay people, and those with special needs were butchered because they were seen as less than human. *Untermensch*, the term that the Nazis used for the non-Aryans, meant that these others were literally sub-human. Is there no redress for all this? Is the smoke from the chimneys of Auschwitz the final answer, as it was meant to be in Hitler's Final Solution?

Or take the examples of carers: many take on the task of looking after loved ones with multiple problems: those in their care can be grown adults who are physically strong, possibly violent, some with special needs, some incapable of speaking, needing care for washing, feeding, medicine, exercise, stimulus and emotional support, twenty-four hours a day, seven days a week, 365 days a year. Around the world carers do this day after day.

Or think of medical staff, cleaners, caterers and porters who looked after desperately sick people during the COVID-19 pandemic, often without protective clothing because of the terrible response of governments, and many on a basic wage. They risked their lives for strangers, and many – far too many – died before their time as a result.

Or look at lovers, some straight, some gay, some transgender, who show their real love in old age. While struggling themselves with physical ailments they still manage the shopping, cooking, cleaning and the attentiveness that their spouses and partners need all the more as they get old.

The Irish poet, Eavan Boland, who died in 2020, has a poem about sacrifice and love:

In the worst hour of the worst season
 of the worst year of a whole people
a man set out from the workhouse with his
    wife.
He was walking – they were both walking
    – north.

She was sick with famine fever and could
    not keep up.
 He lifted her and put her on his back.
He walked like that west and west and
    north.
Until at nightfall under freezing stars they
    arrived.

In the morning they were both found dead.

Of cold. Of hunger. Of the toxins of a
whole history.
But her feet were held against his
breastbone.
The last heat of his flesh was his last gift
to her.

Let no love poem ever come to this
threshold.
There is no place here for the inexact
praise of the easy graces and sensuality of
the body.
There is only time for this merciless
inventory:

Their death together in the winter of 1847.
Also what they suffered. How they lived.
And what there is between a man and
woman.
And in which darkness it can best be
proved.[2]

Is the love that she describes so beautifully simply
projection and wish-fulfilment: we want a future
for the couple, so we invent one? Of course the

2   Eavan Boland, 'Quarantine', *New Collected Poems,* Manchester:
    Carcanet Press, 2008. Reproduced by kind permission of Eavan
    Boland and Carcanet Press.

ideas that we have of God and of an afterlife are greatly influenced by what we want to happen. So, maybe they are all a fiction, but maybe not. There are many things that I want in life and I build great fantasies around them. Some of these turn out to be completely unreal, but others turn out to be real, although in ways that often differ greatly from my fantasies. My projections, which certainly exist, tell us nothing one way or the other about the reality of a next life.

A different view is that the drive towards the ultimate in Eavan Boland's lovers is simply a piece of leftover evolutionary debris that disappears into the ether. Their love is ultimately stimulus and response, like a dog salivating for food, or a comfort blanket that they throw over themselves to hide the emptiness of death. Or maybe we are simply higher animals.

Perhaps so. Perhaps we need to grow up and accept the reality that Hobbes was right: Our lives are 'solitary, poor, nasty, brutish, and short' (*Leviathan*, 1651).

Or perhaps not. Animals do not love like the lovers in Boland's poems. Nor do they write poetry like her. Perhaps instead the husband and wife are images of what it is to be human, made in the image and the likeness of love itself.

No one will be convinced that there can be anything beyond the visible silence of death by arguments. No one fell in love on the basis of sensible reasons. But if we could hear what Mary heard, and hear it in the way that she heard it – perhaps like a baby listening to a mother whispering sweet nothings in her ear – then we might see things differently.

Perhaps the one word spoken by the Gardener, recognised by Mary and passed on by her, did in fact shatter all the final solutions and introduce something utterly wonderful into the world. Perhaps all the heroism, sacrifice and beauty is part of an infinitely greater canvas being painted by one far greater than us. Perhaps brutal injustice is being confronted not by more brutality, but by something far harder to endure when we are confronted by it: the overwhelming love revealed in the voice of the Gardener. In the end the voice confronts us with a choice: to listen to the whispers or to stay within the limits of our sight.

The Now

As it happens, thinking about her own afterlife would *not* have been top of Mary's agenda. She was called to be a disciple. That meant following the Gardener. Before his death the Gardener, had not talked much about the next life. He had never shown any great interest in heaven. He was interested in two things. The first was his Abba, who was not only in heaven, but was present to him now. The second was the new world of relationships that he wanted us to bring about. This was not in the next life. It was in this life – now. It was this present world that absorbed him.

PART 3

THE SIGNIFICANCE OF MARY'S STORY

The story of Mary and the Gardener has given deep comfort to millions of people for over two millennia. In it they see a hope for the future, a life beyond brutality and oppression, a beauty that overcomes despair.

Social Relationships

Many find it easy to connect a story like this with their personal lives. They remember the agony of bereavement, the dark moments of depression, times when life held no meaning for them, their fear and vulnerability as they faced the loneliness of old age. In any of these situations the miracle of the Gardener overcoming death gives us hope, and hope is something we all need desperately.

Praying about Mary and the Gardener can bring us closer to the Gardener. But this is only part of the story. Their relationship is central, but there is more than this. If we stay at the level of two people in their relationship we miss so much else that is important. Not only that, but we face the danger of separating ourselves from God.

The reason for this is that the story does not take place in a vacuum. It is part of the long story of love between Yahweh and the Chosen People. This is often about Yahweh and individuals like Moses, but it is also about Yahweh relating to all the people, not only to individuals.

While the story is about interpersonal relationships it is also about *social relationships*. These are at the centre of the way in which people connect to Yahweh. If the people get these wrong they break the connection with Yahweh. That is why the Gardener said when he was alive: 'Not everyone who says to me, "Lord, Lord", will enter the Kingdom of Heaven, but only the one who does the will of my Father in Heaven' (Matthew 7:21).

So, while the story challenges us at the level of how we personally relate to the Gardener, it also raises questions about how we relate to others in the world around us.

The message brought by Mary to the men was that the Gardener was alive; that the Father had raised him up. This changed the apparent total defeat of the cross into a victory: victory for the message and the values of the Gardener, including his focus on social relationships when he was alive.

Take the example of two men who go to communion each Sunday in the same church. Each has – as he sees it – a warm, good relationship with God, but one has earned $24 billion in the past year. (This is the reported increase in the value of shares held by Jeff Bezos, owner of Amazon and the *Washington Post* in the first few months of the COVID-19 crisis in 2020.[3] The amount is in *billions* not millions. Let's assume that one of our imaginary men was in the same situation.) Let's assume that the second man gets £5000 a year (approximately the rate of basic universal credit in the UK), or €9,000 a year (the approximate basic supplementary welfare allowance for an adult over twenty-five in the Republic of Ireland). Neither man sees a problem with this. The rich man thinks that he has earned his money because he is smart and has made good investments. The second man probably agrees, and wishes that he was a bit smarter himself.

Both are wrong. The rich man was certainly helped by being shrewd in his investments. He

3   Kenya Evelyn, 'Amazon CEO Jeff Bezos grows fortune by $24bn amid coronavirus pandemic', *The Guardian*, 15/04/2020.

was also hugely helped by a financial system that benefits the super-rich. Both were also wrong to receive the Body of Christ without asking questions about their relationship – including their financial relationship – with each other and with the wider Body of Christ.

When he was alive, the Gardener told a good story about this situation: the rich man and Lazarus (Luke 16:19–31). The rich man dies and goes to Hades, whereas the poor man, Lazarus, is brought into the bosom of Abraham. We are not told that the rich man did any harm to Lazarus, who was left at the gate. The rich man may even have thrown him a few coins every day. He didn't do any positive harm to him: he just ignored him for the most part. The focus of the story is on the simple reality that the rich man was rich while Lazarus was poor. He was left being licked by the dogs.

If we read the gospel stories as simply comforting us on a personal level we miss much of their point. The new community that the Gardener wanted was one of respectful relationships. That certainly includes our personal relationship with him. But just as his Jewish people could only relate to Yahweh if they were respectful in their social relationships, so also we can only relate to the Gardener in the same way. Our God is a lover, a lover of *everyone*. That is why asking questions about our financial, social, work, family, gender and other relationships is important. To read the gospel stories and to ignore these is to break our relationship with God. Both our pious Mass attenders in the above example did this: the rich man because he thought it was okay to have an obscene amount of wealth while the poor man beside him struggled; the poor man because he did not realise that the God he was receiving in Christ is a God of justice, and the God of justice is appalled when God's brothers or sisters suffer injustice.

We may legitimately disagree about the means to ensure that our financial and other systems allow people to live in just social relationships. However, it is not legitimate to defend an outcome that leaves some with huge wealth and others in huge poverty, such as we have in today's world. Indeed, one can and should ask: why do people want so much money?

The COVID-19 crisis of 2020–2021 at least brought pressure on the powers-that-be to face the unreality of the structures of injustice that they uphold: structures that crucified people as well as the planet, and left care workers with a basic wage to look after our older loved ones without personal protection equipment. So also, some found to their surprise that some of those who saved their lives in the health service when they were sick were migrants. This should have challenged those who supported wars in countries like Syria – wars that led directly to hundreds of thousands fleeing for their lives – and then scapegoated those who fled.

Women Leaders

Mary's story also raises a different social issue: the role of women leaders in the Church.

Catholic Church rules are clear about the role of women in the governance of the Church. Behind these rules lies a way of understanding the Scriptures, tradition and the Church. In this view women have a very important role, in some ways higher than that of men: it is to imitate Mary of Nazareth, mother and virgin. She was never a priest in the New Testament, but she occupies a place of honour equalled by that of no other woman or man. Her key role during her life on earth was as mother of the Saviour. Now her key role is as mother of us all. In this view, then, women are called to imitate Mary as mother and to follow her faith in accepting the will of God. In Mary women can find someone who understands their suffering as mothers, because she herself suffered at the Cross.

According to this view, the Gardener called twelve apostles during his life: they were all men. At the Last Supper he gave us the gift of the Eucharist, and ordained the first priests, all men. If he had wanted to make women priests, so the argument goes, he would have done so. This he did not do, so the role of women, in this respect, can never change. Throughout the New Testament it was men who were the leaders. Gender roles in the Church have never changed. Nor can they now: that would be unfaithful to the tradition handed down to us.

This view is itself deeply influenced by the way that people see gender roles in the wider society. In a traditional view women are seen as mothers, homemakers, gentle, kind, understanding, the guardians of morality, comforters of men and obedient to the decisions of men who are charged – because of a natural order – with being decision-makers. It is a view that has lost ground in the face of feminism, but elements of it still remain: it is usually women, not men, who make sandwiches at funeral wakes; it is seen as natural that men and only men are priests; it is right, or natural, to defer to the authority of priests because not only are they male, but being celibates who have given their lives to God they are therefore holier than the rest of us; besides, one could not have women priests because they would not keep confidences. Would you want to go to confession to a woman?

The above is a caricature. It seems like something from the past. But it is a view that is still influential.

A key error of this view is to see Mary of Nazareth's primary role as being the mother of the rabbi. But this was not the view of the Gardener. For him, her primary task, in common with all his followers, was to be a disciple. Her calling to be a mother came from her first calling to be a faithful disciple.

Gender roles have changed in wider society, and it is not surprising that these changes have impacted on how women are seen within the Church: the Church will always be influenced by the society in which it exists. However, Christians should not base decisions on these roles on social trends. Instead they should be based on what we can glean from the Scriptures about the values of the Gardener, and how these should be applied to our own time.

If we take the Scriptures seriously we cannot ignore the fact that in the story of Mary and the Gardener the Gardener chose a woman, not a man, as the first to bring to the world the most important news that has ever been spoken. Gender roles within the Church, like those in society, have changed over the centuries in different times and places and we need to ask if these changes are appropriate in the light of what we know about the values of the Gardener.

Gender Roles in the New Testament

John's Gospel presents women as central characters in many of his stories: Mary of Nazareth (at Cana and at the Cross), the Samaritan woman at the well, the woman taken in adultery that the men wanted to stone after they had used her, Mary and Martha of Bethany, his mother's sister, and Mary the wife of Clopas.

The writer of John's Second Letter addressed it to an unnamed woman, 'the dear lady and her children'. Some think that this is a reference to a local church, but it can be argued that since his Third Letter is addressed to an individual, so also is his Second Letter. In his letter to the woman, John asks her to bar people from the house-church, if they do not stay with the faith of Christ. Clearly the unnamed woman had the power to decide whom to bar and whom to welcome.

The other gospel writers also name women in their resurrection stories. Matthew, Mark and Luke name Mary as the first to whom the Gardener appeared. Matthew refers also to 'the other Mary'. Luke names as well Mary the mother of James, Joanna 'and other women'. Given that the appearance of the Gardener after his death was the central belief of his followers, it is not credible to conclude that some if not all these women were *not* leaders in their respective house-churches.

Apart from the gospels, Paul's writings (and his letters date from much earlier: around AD 50) confirm this prominence of women. He does not reference any appearances to women by name, mentioning only that the Gardener appeared to Peter, and then to all Twelve apostles, then to 500 others (who would presumably have included women), then to James (1 Corinthians 15:5–7). However, in some of his other letters he refers to women in ways that suggest they were leaders.

He names his friend Phoebe, who served the

Church at Cenchreae; Prisca or Priscilla, married to Aquila, with whom he stayed a year while in Rome; Junia, whom he calls an 'apostle', and other women leaders (Romans 16:1, 3, 7). In Colossians he mentions Nympha, in whose house the Church meets (Colossians 4:15). Later, Ignatius of Antioch greets two women by name, Tavia and Alce.[4] Fifty years later Alce is mentioned again in the *Martyrdom of Polycarp* (17:2).[5]

The fact that women are singled out for mention in these letters suggests that they were leaders in the communities to which the letters were addressed. What kind of leaders were they, with what kind of responsibility?

Some were wealthy, like Lydia, who was a merchant in the dye trade, and who had the authority to invite Paul and Timothy to stay with her (Philippians 4:2).

When Paul refers to Priscilla and her husband he usually puts her name first. This was very unusual and points to her prominence in the Church.

He refers to Junia and her husband as 'apostles'. The term is used in different senses in the New

4   *Letter to the Smyrnaeans,* chapter 13.
5   Elisabeth Schüssler Fiorenza, *In Memory of Her: A Feminist Reconstruction of Christian Origins*, New York: Crossroad, 1992, p.248.

Testament: it refers to the Twelve whom the rabbi chose, but Paul later calls himself an apostle, and Barnabas is also called an apostle, as are Titus (2 Corinthians 8:23) and Epaphroditus (Philippians 2:25). In any case, an apostle was surely a prominent leader in the community.

Paul mentions roles for some of these women, and these differ from the roles he uses for some men. He refers to Timothy, Titus and Tychichus as his 'helpers' or 'assistants'. This suggest that Paul was their leader. But he refers to Prisca as his 'co-worker', Phoebe as his 'deacon', Junia as his 'apostle'.[6] He tells the Corinthians to be 'subject to every co-worker and labourer' (1 Corinthians 16:16 ff). He uses the same term, 'to labour', or 'to toil', to describe his own work and that of the women. In Romans 16:6, 12 he commends a group of women for having 'laboured hard' for the Lord. He worries that dissensions between Euodia and Syntyche in Philippi will do great damage. It is unlikely that this would have been a major problem unless they were leaders in that Church (Philippians 4:2–3).

Paul himself was clearly a major leader in the early Church. But this Church was made up of many small house-churches. The role models of

6   ibid, p.169.

women and their capacity to be leaders seem to have varied from house-church to house-church, and from time to time. In other parts of the New Testament, for example in Colossians 3:18–4:1, Paul lays down rules for how women are to behave, for example by obeying their husbands. Even if the authorship of Colossians is disputed it shows that different structures of authority operated in different places.

It is often argued today that women have never been leaders in the Church. From the above it seems very unlikely that this was the case.

Gender Roles in Society

At one level, the leadership exercised by these women is not surprising. During the first century, in wider Roman and Greek society, women in cities were magistrates and priestesses, for example in the pagan temple of Artemis in Ephesus. The Acts of the Apostles refers to this temple (Acts 19:24). In Jewish as well as pagan communities women could also hold prominent posts: a tomb inscription in Syria, dating from the second or third centuries, refers to Rufina, who was president of the synagogue. In Gentile society women also had some power: we are told in Acts 13:52 that the Jews in Antioch in Pisidia stirred up 'Gentile women of high social standing' to join them in expelling Paul and Barnabas from the city.

Gender roles have also changed dramatically in Ireland in the past fifty years. One has only to remember that women in Ireland remained the chattels (the legal possessions) of their husband up to recent times.

In my own family my mother got a BA from University College Dublin, then entered the Civil Service, but had to retire on marriage. Society expected her to have her husband's lunch ready for him from then on (so did he). This she did, but managed some entrepreneurial business on the side. One of my sisters became a nurse and ended up teaching nursing. She had been taught domestic science in school, and had done no science despite her academic ability. It is worth noting that I was in my forties before it occurred to me that she became a nurse and not a doctor because she was a woman. In the third generation, one of my nieces became a professor in a major hospital: she had studied applied maths in school.

The experiences of these three women were greatly influenced, if not actually determined, by society's expectations, especially in regard to gender roles, which in turn influenced their different education. Similar stories of this change in options open to succeeding generations could be told by many families in Ireland.

Working-class women, with reduced economic choices, suffered even more from the boxes into which they were put because of their gender.

A striking change for all women in Ireland is that the appalling practice of condemning single women who are pregnant to institutions no longer takes place, and while economic and other barriers still make it difficult for many to leave abusive husbands, others are able to do so far more than in the past.

Women Leaders in Today's Church

The leadership of women in the early Church is in marked contrast to the absolute exclusion of women from the main leadership roles in the modern Church. Visually, the absence of women among cardinals and bishops processing into major meetings in Rome, presided over by a monarchical figure (however much Pope Francis has tried to modify this) is very striking. Not only are they men but the vast majority have not been elected by their church community. Not only that, but women – and lay men – are explicitly excluded from leadership roles in the Church by canon 129.

Pope Francis has been a marvellous breath of fresh air in the Church. He has spoken about the need for an enhanced role for women in society: 'Women have the right to be actively involved in all areas, and their right must be asserted and protected even by legal means wherever they prove necessary.' This must take place, he said, at local, national and international levels, 'as well as the ecclesial'.[7] However, he has been slow to appoint women to key positions in the Vatican curia. The 2020 appointment of Francesca Di Giovanni as Undersecretary for Relations with States in the Secretariat of State was notable because it was the highest such appointment for a woman. Clearly Francis faces much opposition in doing more, but this simply highlights the depth of patriarchy that exists in the Church.

An argument used to justify this is that the rabbi never ordained women. There is a double argument here. One is that only the ordained can exercise authority in the Church. The second is that only men can get ordained, so only men can exercise

7   Speech to members of the Pontifical Council for Interreligious Dialogue, 9 June 2017.

authority. Both arguments are false.

In response to the argument that women cannot be priests because the Gardener ordained only men, Kieran O'Mahony, Biblical Studies Coordinator in the archdiocese of Dublin, is one of a long line of scholars who point out that the rabbi ordained no one at the Last Supper. He argues that the historical rabbi never foresaw the development of a church separate from his own Jewish religion. He saw himself as sent 'to the lost tribes of the house of Israel', so he never thought about setting up ministries for a new Church.

> This means that the historical Jesus 'ordained' nobody at all and the Last Supper was not an ordination service, simply because the historical Jesus did not reckon with a body separate from his own Jewish faith. As a result, the argument from the Last Supper that only men can be ordained makes no sense.[8]

Instead different ministries began to emerge as the early followers of the Gardener – who at first

---

8   Kieran O'Mahony, Letter to the Editor, *The Tablet*, 29 February 2020.

were mostly Jews – were expelled from the Jewish synagogues. These new roles emerged in response to the needs of the community. So, we read in the Acts of the Apostles that seven deacons were selected to deal fairly with the distribution of food because of tensions among the Jewish and Gentile members of the new community. These deacons were all men, but elsewhere, as we have seen, women were referred to as deacons. O'Mahony argues that this development of ministries was guided by the Spirit of the Gardener, and that we should be open to the same Spirit guiding us today.[9]

There were no cardinals in the New Testament. That in itself is not an argument against the role: if there is a need for it then we should have it. It is, however, an argument against requiring all cardinals to be ordained. Historically they were often lay people. In some cases they were young nephews of the pope. The requirement for ordination was introduced by John XXIII. If those opposed to the ordination of women are not biased against women, why do they not call for the appointment of non-ordained people as cardinals, and for the majority to be women? Doing so would be a big gesture towards making the Church a sign of the

9   *The Tablet,* 29 February 2020, p.16.

community that the Gardener wanted to see.

Or, given the shortage of priests in many countries, why are more lay women and men not appointed as administrators of parishes, as happens in some US parishes? Why are married men not ordained priests, given that married Anglicans and Eastern Rite clergy are accepted in the Church?

The improved education of women in the past 150 years, particularly of those who, for many years, have been highly qualified in theology, means that gender roles within the Church have changed enormously. Indeed women often now speak during Mass and other services, although the permission of the male priest is required to allow them to do this.

Officially, women have power and influence in the Church in education, in academia, in charitable and justice organisations, but they have no authority to decide how the Eucharist should be celebrated, or what should be preached and how, or who should be appointed as parish priest, bishop or pope, or on Church teaching on any issue, including birth control and abortion, or in relation to finance. The same, of course, is true of lay men. Most priests, indeed, have very limited, if any, influence over the appointment of priests and other officials.

A particular issue is that women chaplains in hospitals accompany their patients, often over several years, as they go through the difficult journey of terminal illness. Yet, towards the end, when patients ask for it, women chaplains are barred from giving them the Sacraments of Reconciliation or of the Sick. They have to seek the services of a man who may have had no contact with the patient. This is not sensible. There is a theological vision behind the rules that leads to this outcome. When theology leads to a bad outcome, it should be re-examined.

The Church's purpose, the very reason for its existence, is to follow the example of its Founder. Yet the Gardener chose a woman as his first apostle – apostle in the sense of one who is sent out to bring a message to others. Later Mary would be called the 'apostle of the apostles' by Thomas Aquinas, and the phrase was used of her by John Paul II, and in Pope Francis's 2016 decree changing her memorial to a feast day.[10] It is particularly striking that until this decree, Mary had no feast day; instead she had an optional memorial which meant that priests could choose whether or not to give her special

10 'Mary Magdalene, apostle of the apostles', Holy See Press Office, 10/06/2016.

prominence. The one who was commissioned by the Gardener had been reduced to the same rank as thousands of other saints in our calendar. As a follower of the Gardener Mary would not have been bothered by this, but it should bother us as a community trying to reflect the values of the Gardener.

Ordaining women may not be the most urgent of changes needed in the church. It is more important to find ways to speak about the Gardener to secular cultures. It is equally important to try to limit the way in which the message of the Gardener is so often used to bolster fundamentalism based on fear or a false need for certainty.

Yet we also need to change all that is involved in clericalism. This is not easy to do. Clericalism is a system. In part it is about Church law, but while laws are important, assumptions and ethos are even more so. For example, when people say that they have problems with a priest's sermon, they seldom tell him. Many lay people still defer to a priest in committees.

Much of this has changed, in part because of the abuse scandals, but much of it still remains.

Our capacity to deal with any of these issues is undermined by the absolute ban on so many church members becoming decision-makers. Discrimination against women is a dark stain on our Church. It undermines our credibility in preaching the message of the Gardener, precisely because this discrimination is in direct opposition to his message.

Geoffrey Arrand, a retired Anglican priest, remarked in a letter to *The Tablet* (21/3/2019) that the arguments in the Roman Catholic Church were familiar to him from *The Church Times* in the 1980s and 1990s. He suspected that the outcome, however long and bitter, will be the same as it was in the Church of England.

Appointing women leaders in the Church is not something that should be done because it is popular; or to meet demands for women's rights – although that is important – or in the hope that doing so will fill our pews – it may well do the opposite – or that women will be better leaders than men – they will probably be the same mixture of saints and scoundrels, geniuses and incompetents that men are. Instead, women should be invited to take on leadership roles because this is what the Gardener did, and it should be done so that the Church should not symbolise values opposed to those of the Gardener, but instead be a symbol of his respect for all and his desire to include all.

As a community, members of the Catholic Church will continue to disagree about the role of women: that is not surprising. If we did not have serious disagreements, we would not be Catholic, because Catholic means universal. Instead we would be a small cult of like-minded people. In the end, what matters most may not be the different positions that we hold on issues like this, but *how* we handle our disagreements.

Were we to start our discussions on contentious issues by focusing on the story of Mary and the Gardener we might handle them better. We might ask what was going on in Mary? What did she think of her role as an apostle? What was going on in the mind of the Gardener when he chose a woman to be the first person to reveal the Good News that he had overcome death, and to be his first messenger to his brothers?

PART 4

MARY, THE GARDENER, AND TODAY

Mary's story is a glimpse into the life of the early followers of the Gardener before and after his death. The resurrection stories are stories of people filled with fear and hopelessness, dispersed and utterly despondent, becoming people who were courageous and enthusiastic and who acted together as a group. The cause of this change was their relationship with the Gardener after his death.

Personal

Mary's relationship with the Gardener after his death was born out of her name being spoken. We do not recognise people who speak our name unless we know them well. We are not told anything more about the relationship from then on.

In later history Mary is often depicted as a prostitute. This was because driving seven demons out of her was interpreted sexually and because the woman washing the feet of the rabbi was seen as a penitent sinner (although, again, her sins may have had nothing to do with sex). None of the texts support this interpretation. The view of Mary as a prostitute was highlighted by Pope Gregory 1 (23rd homily). He conflated Luke's sinful woman with the woman who anointed the rabbi's feet and with Mary of Bethany, and then argued that the story of the seven devils driven out of Mary was about curing her of prostitution. The tradition was further strengthened by medieval paintings of her as a prostitute. That tradition was never accepted by the Eastern Church.

Perhaps Mary was a prostitute. This would not have stopped the Gardener both relating to her and calling her to follow him. He did not shun sexual sinners, but he challenged the self-righteous when they condemned women, without also pointing the finger at men, as we see in the story of how he dealt with the accusers of the adulteress in John 8:1–11: 'Let anyone among you who is without sin be the first to throw a stone at her'. We are told that the men left one by one, starting with the oldest. But the texts do not point to Mary being a prostitute, so why should we continue the tradition?

The Gardener had healed Mary of seven devils,

whatever illness that refers to. But he had done more: by revealing himself to her he had deepened her relationship with him beyond measure. And by giving her a mission he had changed her from being a passive receiver of gifts to being an active leader in her community, one driven by the love she had received to help others to experience that same love and freedom.

Communal

The personal relationship that Mary had with the Gardener was intense, but it was not only personal, it was also communal: she was part of a community. That community was made up of many smaller communities, and in all of them that we know about divisions were rife. The greatest division was over the regulations to be imposed on Gentiles who joined the community, which initially was mostly made up of Jews. Should Gentile men be required to accept circumcision? Should all of them be required to accept Jewish dietary laws? The row, and its working out, is described in the Acts of the Apostles, chapter 15, and is often referred to by Paul in his letters. For him, a central point was that we cannot be made right with God by following rules, but only by faith in Christ. 'Faith' here means something like the trusting relationship that the Gardener showed towards his Father on the cross.

There is no mention of Mary playing a role in this particular dispute. She may well have been dead by the time of the dispute. However, as a leader in the Church she would have had to deal with other conflicts and to find ways to resolve them.

Conflict is part of any human group. What matters is how we handle it and respond to it. Conflict is also difficult. That is why it is so tempting to focus on our personal relationship with God and stay far away from the community. This is all the more the case when the community has as many unattractive aspects as the Roman Catholic Church has today.

Nonetheless, the exclusive me-and-Jesus approach is a temptation for the Christian. Important as my personal relationship with the Lord is my relationship with the wider community is at least as important. Had Mary spent the rest of her life after the meeting in the garden focusing only on her personal relationship with the Gardener we would never have heard of her. She would not have been a leader in the community. She would not have fulfilled the mission given to her by the Gardener to go to the male disciples.

In practice she would have denied the whole approach of God to the chosen people: Yahweh called them as a *people*. Moses was invited into a deep personal relationship with Yahweh, but he was also sent to lead his people to freedom. He was asked to challenge Pharaoh and his might. When he protested that he could not do this because he could not even speak well, he was told that the power of Yahweh would be with him. Mary, too, was sent to free the Gardener's people: and that includes everyone born into the world.

Discipleship

The key response that the Gardener looks for in those who follow him is *discipleship*. This certainly involves an intense personal relationship with him, but it also means working for freedom within ourselves and seeking freedom for others. Following him means joining in the mission that he himself was called to fulfil by his Father:

> The Spirit of the Lord is upon me because he has anointed me to bring good news to the poor. He has sent me to proclaim release to the captives and recovery of sight to the blind. (Luke 4:18)

It was not a new mission: scr, as a pious Jew, was quoting Isaiah 61:1–2. It was the same mission given to the Chosen People: to set my people free.

Discipleship was more important to the Gardener than family relationships. We see this in the story in Mark 3 where he is told that his mother and brothers are outside the house looking for him. They are there because they think he has gone mad, and also because his madness in criticising religious and political authorities is endangering their lives as well as his own. His response is to point to the people in the room and ask, 'Who are my mother and brothers and sisters? Those who do the will of God' (Mark 3:20–35).

It is not surprising that there was tension between the Gardener and his family: as an adult he had worked as a carpenter, or builder. His earnings would have been important for the extended family who, while not at the bottom of the economic pile, would certainly have struggled to make ends meet, including paying taxes. They would surely not have been pleased at his decision to give up his work and head off into the desert to search for God. Nonetheless he persisted in his decision to seek God first in the desert, and later among the people in the small villages in Palestine.

So, when we speak of Mary's friendship with the Gardener the key element in it must have been discipleship. Being a disciple involved friendship, spending time with the Gardener, going to frequent meals with him, enjoying his laughter, sitting listening to him, and wondering about him. But it also meant watching him spend long hours in prayer to his Father, worrying about the trouble he was getting into with his challenges of the powers-that-be, hearing him talk about suffering and death, and calling his disciples to follow him on his way of the cross.

After her meeting with him in the garden, discipleship sent Mary on her mission to the men. Later, as a leader of the new community it surely brought her into the centre of the conflicts within the community and with those who were outsiders, and she, like the others, presumably had to bear the brunt of persecution. In all this she faced a challenge similar to that of the Gardener: could she be faithful to his life-filled vision, his hope and his final trust in his Father?

The fact that all the gospels refer to her suggests that she remained a leader up to her death, and this in turn suggests that in fact she was faithful to her Gardener until the end.

Today

Discipleship has to be worked out within the Church today: opposing clericalism, ending patriarchy, respecting gender difference, challenging the prevalent middle-class bias within the Church, welcoming refugees, and trying to be open to the marvellous richness of what is being offered by the Gardener.

That task of opening up the Word needs the scholarship of theologians from our own and other Churches, the leadership of Church officials, the dedication of the millions working with the marginalised, often in work entirely hidden from the wider world; and it also needs the wisdom and experience of lay people, men and women, being included seriously in the community's discernment about all Church issues, including the development of doctrine.

The mission also has a focus on those suffering injustice. People cannot live in freedom if they do not have food, or if they are subject to domestic or child abuse, or if they are swamped by consumerism, or choking because of terrible air quality, or drowning in floods, or dying because of curable disease. It is surely blasphemy to come to receive the Lord in the Eucharist without showing concern for our brothers and sisters in the Lord.

Mary's mission, in Luke's version, failed: the men ignored her. However, her mission did not end with that failure, any more than the Gardener's mission ended because of the defeat of his dreams on the cross. She continued to lead the community.

If she had not done so, they would not have given her such a prominent place in their story of the Gardener, stories written about forty to fifty years after the event.

The word spoken to Mary – her name – meant that the brutality of the crucifixion was not the last word; that the apparent abandonment on the cross, 'My God, my God, why have you forsaken me?' was not the end; that the dreams for a new world that the Gardener had spoken about during his life were not dead; that the deep relationship with the disciples was not over.

In the end the sheer power of the love of God, revealed in and by the Gardener, and brought from him to the world by Mary, has and will overcome evil.

One word had transformed the world:

'Mary'.

¹¹ Now Mary stood outside the tomb crying. As she wept, she bent over to look into the tomb ¹² and saw two angels in white, seated where Jesus' body had been, one at the head and the other at the foot.

¹³ They asked her, 'Woman, why are you crying?'

'They have taken my Lord away,' she said, 'and I don't know where they have put him.'

¹⁴ At this, she turned around and saw Jesus standing there, but she did not realise that it was Jesus.

¹⁵ He asked her, 'Woman, why are you crying? Who is it you are looking for?'

Thinking he was the gardener, she said, 'Sir, if you have carried him away, tell me where you have put him, and I will get him.'

¹⁶ Jesus said to her, 'Mary'.

She turned toward him and cried out in Aramaic, 'Rabboni!' (which means 'Teacher').

¹⁷ Jesus said, 'Do not hold on to me, for I have not yet ascended to the Father.

Go instead to my brothers and tell them, "I am ascending to my Father and your Father, to my God and your God.'"

¹⁸ Mary of Magdala went to the disciples with the news: 'I have seen the Lord!' And she told them that he had said these things to her.

John 20: 11–18
(New International Version).